THE PROBLEM WITH MOISTURE

HUMIDITY FOR KIDS

SCIENCE BOOK AGE 7

Children's Science & Nature Books

Speedy Publishing LLC
40 E. Main St. #1156
Newark, DE 19711
www.speedypublishing.com

On some days, everything feels a little damp. Where does that water come from? Let's do a deep dive into moisture and humidity!

WHAT HUMIDITY IS

Although the air around us usually looks clear, it is not empty. Along with the oxygen and other gases that make up our atmosphere there are floating particles of dust, smoke, tree pollen—and water.

In fact there is a lot of water in the air, in the form of vapor. We can't see it, but often we can feel it, or the lack of it.

WINDOW GLASS WITH CONDENSATION

When we talk about the water in the air when it's not raining or snowing, we refer to it as humidity. The humidity is rising when the amount of water in the atmosphere around us increases.

MEASURING HUMIDITY

Humidity is how much water vapor, or moisture, is in the air. We measure it in grams of moisture in a cubic meter of air, or g/m3.

There are two main scales for measuring humidity:

- Absolute Humidity
- Relative Hyumidity

HUMIDITY
100
90
80
70
60

ABSOLUTE HUMIDITY:

This reports the amount of water in a volume of air. But to know what this means, we also have to know the temperature of the air, as warmer air can hold more water vapor than colder air.

For example, if the temperature is 30°C/86°F, a cubic meter of air can hold as much as 30 grams of water vapor, or 30g/m3. But if it's a cold day and the temperature is at the freezing point (0°C/32°F), a cubic meter of air can only hold about 5 grams of water vapor: 5g/m3.

°C
°F
50
40
30
20
10
0
10
20
30
120
100
80
60
40
20
0
20

RELATIVE HUMIDITY:

Relative humidity takes temperature into account. It tells us the amount of water vapor in the air compared to the maximum the air could hold at the current temperature. We usually express this as a percentage: the actual humidity divided by the absolute humidity for the temperature.

WEATHER FORECAST

Weather forecasters usually use relative humidity in their reports because it is a more useful figure. If you hear that the relative humidity is 92 percent, then no matter whether it is warm or cold, you know it may rain or snow later in the day. If the relative humidity is 5 percent, no matter what the temperature is you can leave your umbrella at home.

WHAT HUMIDITY CAN DO

Even if the relative humidity is high, it does not guarantee there will be rain or snow. Other factors like wind and differences in temperature at different altitudes can come into play. However, if the relative humidity gets to 100 percent—the air is holding all the moisture it can hold at the current temperature—there is one sure result: dew.

BEAUTIFUL SHINY DEW DROPS ON A DANDELION SEED

Dew is water condensing out of the air because there is more than the air can hold. So another weather forecaster term is the "dew point".

CLOSEUP DEW DROPS

The dew point works like this: let's say that right now it is a warm day and relatively humid, with the relative humidity around 70 percent.

As the day gets cooler and if nothing else changes, the relative humidity will climb because the cooler air can hold a smaller volume of water vapor than the warmer air could.

When the temperature drops far enough the air will have cooled so that—although the amount of water has not changed—the cooler air can no longer hold it all and dew starts forming. That temperature is the dew point for the humidity in that place at that time.

Most people feel comfortable with a dew-point temperature up to 60°F (16°C). As the dew point climbs to around 70°F (21°C), people begin to feel sticky and too hot. There is so much water vapor in the air around the person that the perspiration or even sweat the person is generating in order to get cooler has no place to go! The dew point, along with how much wind there is, whether it is a clear or cloudy day, and where the sun is in the sky have a lot to do with how comfortable we feel.

The humidity in the air comes from water evaporating. Most of that water does not come from people sweating, but from the surface of lakes and oceans. The Earth is warmer nearer the equator than it is at the poles, so the air at the equator can absorb more water vapor than Arctic air can, and nearer the equator is also where the most evaporation happens.

EVAPORATION

CARIBBEAN OCEAN

The most humid air masses in the atmosphere tend to be near warm bodies of water, like the Caribbean Ocean, the Persian Gulf, and the Red Sea. The air over a desert can have a very high capacity for humidity, but there is just not that much water vapor around for the air to receive. This means the relative humidity over the desert may be near 1 percent.

HUMIDITY CHALLENGES

Extremes of humidity can cause problems for people and for the things around them. These challenges are the following:

- Discomfort
- Health Risks

TOO MUCH HEAT CAN CAUSE DISCOMFORT

DISCOMFORT

As noted earlier, we cool down our bodies by perspiration and sweating. If the relative humidity is low, that moisture has somewhere to go, and as it evaporates into the air around us, we feel cooler. But if the relative humidity is high, the moisture on our skin evaporates much less quickly and we cool down much more slowly. We can feel sticky and overheated.

On the other hand, if the relative humidity is extremely low, the air around you may start drawing more moisture out of your skin than is good for you. Even if the temperature is not particularly hot, your skin may start feeling dry and may even start cracking.

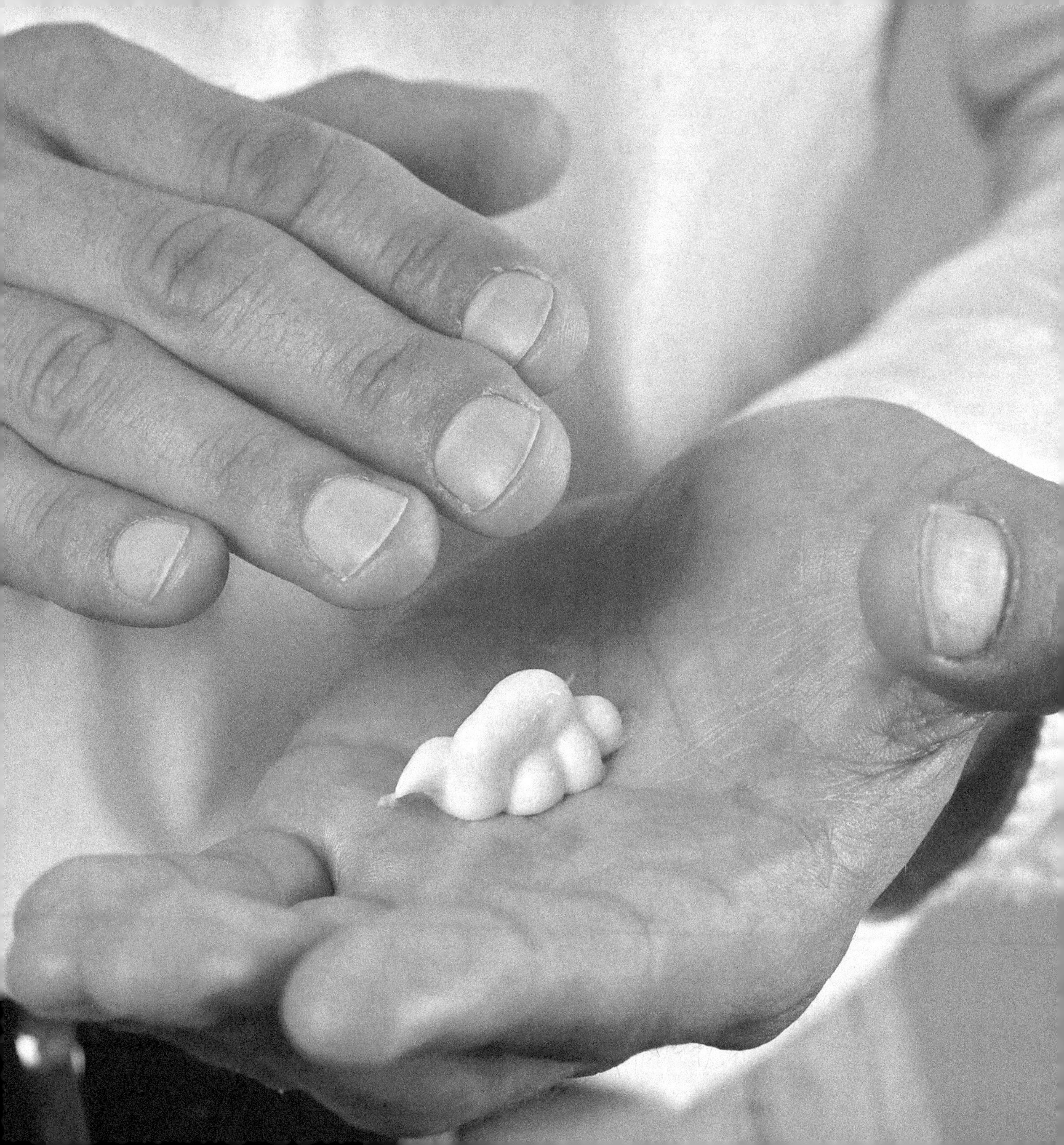

TOO MUCH HEAT CAN CAUSE HEAT STROKE

HEALTH RISKS

Beyond comfort, it you are involved in activities in extremely high or low humidity, you can cause problems for your body unless you adjust what your are doing. You know to take extra water when it is hot and you are sweating; but you should also drink extra liquids when the relative humidity is very low, to keep up with the water that the air around you is removing from your skin without you even noticing it.

If you are exercising in high relative humidity, be aware of the dew point. The higher the dew point, the more slowly moisture will evaporate and therefore the more slowly you will cool down. In extreme conditions, people who let themselves overheat and cannot find a way to cool down may lose consciousness or could even die.

T STROKE THE DANGER OF WORKING OUT IN THE HOT WEATHER

DAMP PAINT ON THE WALL

AROUND THE HOME

If you live in a house where the relative humidity is always high, you may notice a number of not-nice effects:

- Damages
- Insects
- Molds

DAMAGE CAUSED BY DAMP AND MOISTURE ON A CEILING

Damage: Books, cardboard playing cards, and even the materials the walls are made of can absorb extra moisture from humid air. This can distort and damage the material even if nobody touches it; and if somebody turns the pages of a damp book or tries to shuffle damp playing cards, the edges of the material can become feathered and rippled.

TERMITE CROWD FLYING AROUND LAMP LIGHTING FRONT HOUSE IN DAMP WEATHER

Insects: Small insects are always in danger of dehydrating, because they lose moisture rapidly. That's why they love living in damp places. If you have a damp place in your house—perhaps a bath mat that's left on the floor in front of the shower for a few days—you may find that you have created an ideal habitat for various creepy bugs that you don't want to have around you.

Mold: Mold spores need moisture to grow. When they find a damp, warm area, they go to town! Once you get mold in the walls of your house, in your bedding, or in stored clothing or books, it is very hard to get rid of it again.

WINDOW MOLDS

On the other hand, if you keep the relative humidity very low, you can cause a different range of problems, including cracked skin and dry eyes. Bacteria can find a home in a super-dry house, too!

HUMIDITY FUN FACTS

Humidity affects our languages. Our vocal cords are more or less elastic depending on how humid the air is around us. Tonal languages like Chinese and Vietnamese rely on flexible vocal cords to accurately reproduce the tones as well as the sounds of the language. Scientists have found that tonal languages have rarely developed in areas of low humidity.

DIFFERENT LANGUAGES AROUND THE WORLD

WET HAIR

The first measurement of humidity was with hair. A strand of human hair has several layers. The inner layer is filled with keratin proteins that attach to each other. When your hair is wet, the water molecules bridge the gaps between protein molecules.

As your hair dries, it can get wavy or curly as gaps develop between the keratin molecules and the hair bends or folds. In 1783 in Switzerland, a scientist built a tool

for measuring the humidity in the air, using strands of human hair. By measuring how curly the strands of hair became, the scientist could measure how humid the air was.

LEARN ABOUT YOUR HOME PLANET

You were born to live on Earth, and with a little thought you can enjoy almost every part of the planet! You now know to pay attention to humidity.

To learn more about other challenges your planet has to offer you, read Baby Professor books like A Giant Shield: A Study of the Atmosphere and A Kid's Book of Extreme Weather.

www.ingramcontent.com/pod-product-compliance
Lightning Source LLC
LaVergne TN
LVHW060507170826
845677LV00026B/1643

* 9 7 9 8 8 6 9 4 3 2 3 4 6 *